Mr Fuzzypants: Cyber-Safety Star

Story by Suzanne Barton

Illustrations by Ellie O'Shea

Mr Fuzzypants: Cyber-Safety Star

Text: Suzanne Barton
Publishers: Tania Mazzeo and Eliza Webb
Series consultant: Amanda Sutera
  Hands on Heads Consulting
Editor: Sarah Layton
Project editor: Annabel Smith
Designer: Jess Kelly
Project designer: Danielle Maccarone
Illustrations: Ellie O'Shea
Production controller: Renee Tome

NovaStar

Text © 2024 Cengage Learning Australia Pty Limited
Illustrations © 2024 Cengage Learning Australia Pty Limited

ISBN 978 0 17 033421 1

Cengage Learning Australia
Level 5, 80 Dorcas Street
Southbank VIC 3006 Australia
Phone: 1300 790 853
Email: aust.nelsonprimary@cengage.com

For learning solutions, visit **cengage.com.au**

Printed in China by 1010 Printing International Ltd
1 2 3 4 5 6 7 28 27 26 25 24

*Nelson acknowledges the Traditional Owners and Custodians
of the lands of all First Nations Peoples. We pay respect
to Elders past and present, and extend that respect to
all First Nations Peoples today.*

Contents

Chapter 1

A Pesky Poet

"Dodge the T-rex, collect all the crystals and – whatever you do – don't step on the stink moss," Ivy said.

"Easy-peasy," Charlie said, pounding his controller even faster. "We're going to win this race!"

Ivy and Charlie were sitting in the lounge room in front of their gaming console. School was over for the week, and all their friends had logged on remotely to play their favourite online video game – *Dino Speedster*.

On the TV screen, Charlie and Ivy's avatars rode dinosaurs across a magical landscape. They raced through the course, pushing past the other players. They always pushed past the other players.

Charlie sniggered as he typed in the chat box: *Mwahahahaaa! You'll never beat us, slowpokes!*

Their friends replied with emojis.

"There's a huge patch of stink moss right before the finish line!" Ivy said.

"I see it!" Charlie replied. "Jump on the count of three. One, two, three – *jump!*"

The avatars soared through the sky on their dinosaurs. But just as Ivy and Charlie were about to win, the screen went dark!

"What did you do?" Ivy snapped.

"I didn't do anything, what did *you* do?"
Charlie screeched.

Just then, some words appeared on
the screen:

*"I locked your game
        to teach you a lesson.
Kids with weak passwords
        won't keep people guessin'.
So quit the screen and make me lunch.
I'll have some broccoli – thanks a bunch!"*

"What's going on? Who would ruin our game?" Ivy asked.

"And for *broccoli*?" Charlie added, screwing up his nose in disgust.

A squeaky little laugh rang out across the room. Charlie and Ivy turned towards the sound and gasped. Their pet guinea pig, Mr Fuzzypants, was sitting on the coffee table wearing a tiny headset. His paw hovered over a tablet.

Mr Fuzzypants made some squeaks into his microphone and punched some buttons on the tablet. Then he looked up at Charlie and Ivy with his head cocked to one side and he began to "speak" in a robotic-sounding voice.

"I've been watching out for you two online to keep you cyber safe, but it's very difficult when you have such simple game passwords," Mr Fuzzypants said. "I need a break."

Ivy and Charlie looked at each other
in disbelief.

"Besides, it's not nice to call your friends
mean names like slowpokes," Mr Fuzzypants
continued. "Now, how about that broccoli?"

"MUM!" the kids yelled.

Chapter 2

The Amazing Invention

"You've got to see this, Mum!" Ivy squealed. "I think the app you made to translate pet sounds to English *works*."

"No way," Mum said, as she came into the lounge room. "My inventions never work."

It was true. Mum had lots of brilliant ideas, but the house was full of half-finished gadgets – like the Stinkomatic Sock-Cleaning Machine and the very dangerous Hoverboard Step Stool.

Mum picked up Mr Fuzzypants and looked him hard in the eyes as Charlie and Ivy explained what had happened. The guinea pig had wriggled out of his headset and was twitching his nose innocently.

"I think you two have played enough video games for today – you're imagining things," Mum said. "Besides, haven't you got a school project to prepare for?"

"Mr Fuzzypants really *was* talking, and he *can* use a tablet," Charlie said.

"He locked us out of our game to teach us a lesson about cyber safety," Ivy added.

"Very funny," Mum said, putting Mr Fuzzypants down. "Project time!"

Ivy and Charlie slumped onto the couch as Mum left the room.

"What are we going to do?" Charlie asked. "Mum doesn't believe us, and we're still locked out of our game."

"Maybe we did imagine the whole thing," Ivy said. "There's no way a guinea pig could talk, right?"

Mr Fuzzypants was staring at them. It almost looked like he was grinning.

Chapter 3

Shopping Spree

Ding dong. Ding dong. Ding dong.

The next morning, Charlie and Ivy woke to the sound of the front doorbell ringing again and again. They raced down the hall and saw Mum surrounded by loads of parcels, looking confused.

"Do you know anything about this?" Mum asked. "We're getting *a lot* of deliveries."

Charlie and Ivy shook their heads and began to open some of the parcels. Inside, there were vegetables and some fancy mini furniture.

"Weird," Charlie said. "Everything is addressed to Mr Fuzzypants ..."

"And it's all been charged to my credit card," Mum groaned, checking the banking app on her phone.

"Something's nibbled a hole in this one," Ivy said, looking at one box.

Suddenly, a glittering pet exercise ball burst from the top of the chewed box. Mr Fuzzypants was inside the ball, and as he ran it rolled through the house. Charlie, Ivy and Mum chased the guinea pig as he whizzed around at top speed, like he was driving a sports car.

When they finally cornered Mr Fuzzypants in the lounge room, Charlie opened the ball and scooped the guinea pig out onto the coffee table. He was wearing a brand-new tiny tuxedo.

Mr Fuzzypants scurried over to his tablet and wriggled into his headset. After squeaking and tapping on the screen for a moment, he turned to Mum and "spoke" in his robotic voice.

"I hope you don't mind me buying a few treats using your credit card, Linda," Mr Fuzzypants said. "Once I'd guessed the kids' game passwords, it was easy to see all your bank account details."

Mum blinked at the guinea pig, then flopped into a beanbag in shock.

Chapter 4

Enough Is Enough!

Charlie and Ivy fanned Mum as she stared at the talking tech-whizz guinea pig in amazement. Mr Fuzzypants kept squeaking and tapping away on the tablet, then looked up with a satisfied smile.

"The pet-to-English translator is a great invention! It just needed a few small changes," he said. "I've used it to learn about lots of things. So far, I've taken online lessons in cyber safety, coding and poetry."

"That explains why you sent us that silly poem yesterday," Ivy giggled.

Mr Fuzzypants tapped more urgently.

"There's nothing *silly* about cyber safety," he said. "Simple passwords can lead to all sorts of trouble. They need to be much harder to guess than just 'Password123'. You should thank me for this lesson."

Charlie, Ivy and Mum thanked Mr Fuzzypants and promised to make their passwords more difficult.

"Now *please* unlock our video game!" Charlie begged.

"I'm not sure you've learnt your lesson," Mr Fuzzypants said.

Ivy and Charlie moaned, but the guinea pig ignored them and kept talking.

"Besides, you'll be too busy looking after me to play games," Mr Fuzzypants said. "I'm the world's first talking guinea pig. I'm going to be a star! I've already started posting videos on RodentTube."

Just then, Mum glanced out the window. "There's a film crew outside! I think they're talking about a 'celebrity guinea pig'," Mum said. "Enough is enough! How did they find us? Our address is private information."

"Perhaps I have become a little distracted from my goal to teach the world about cyber safety," Mr Fuzzypants said. "But don't worry, I won't forget you when I'm famous, living in my dream house, with a pool full of broccoli soup and –"

Suddenly, Mr Fuzzypants went silent.

"This has gone too far, Mr Fuzzypants,"
Ivy said. "I've turned off the tablet."

The guinea pig had no way to speak.
He twitched his nose in panic.

Ivy placed Mr Fuzzypants back in his hutch
and Charlie hid the headset and tablet.

Then the family sat down for a talk about
why passwords should be hard to guess
and should never be shared.

Mum ordered a new credit card, and Ivy
and Charlie set strong new passwords.
But they still couldn't log in to their game.
Mr Fuzzypants had locked it tight, and he
wasn't in the mood to help.

Chapter 5

A Perfect Pact

Charlie and Ivy decided to do their school project on cyber safety. They started work on a video immediately, but it was hard to concentrate with sad squeaks and sighs coming from the guinea pig hutch.

"Charlie," Ivy said, walking over to Mr Fuzzypants's hutch. "This video is pretty boring so far. Do you know what would make the best presentation *ever*?"

"Do you still want to be a big star, Mr Fuzzypants?" Ivy asked.

Charlie chuckled. The guinea pig's ears pricked up.

"You must promise to use your knowledge for good and to teach all our friends about cyber safety. No online shopping. No RodentTube," Charlie said. "And you have to unlock our game."

Mr Fuzzypants grumbled.

"We promise to be more cyber safe and to be more kind when we're gaming," Ivy said.

"And to give you all our broccoli," Charlie added.

Mr Fuzzypants suddenly leapt up and squeaked with joy.

The next day, Mr Fuzzypants got his wish to be a star.

When Ivy and Charlie played their video at school, everyone was amazed to see that it was hosted by a talking guinea pig. Mr Fuzzypants told jokes, performed silly poems and shared lots of cyber-safety tips.

The teacher even made Mr Fuzzypants a cyber-safety champion and arranged for him to tour around all the schools in the area. Pretty soon, Mr Fuzzypants had lots of fans, who gave him all the treats he could ever desire.

Mr Fuzzypants kept his promise to unlock Charlie and Ivy's game. Protected by strong passwords, the kids could finally race dinosaurs again. They even gave their friends a head start ... sometimes.

CHARLIE You can do it, Emily!

Thanks for the head start! EMILY

IVY Nice one, Tyler.

Woohoo! TYLER